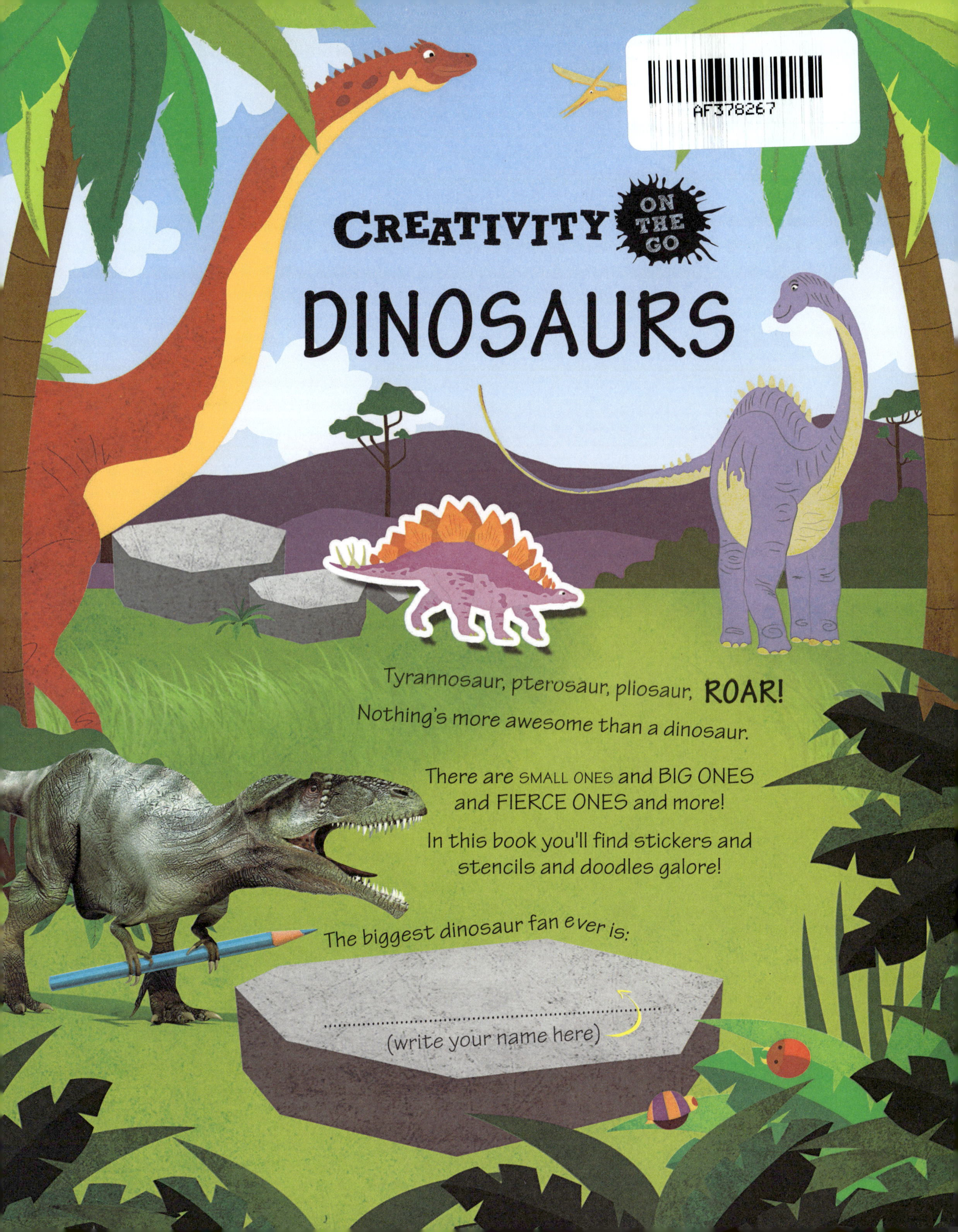

AF378267
CREATIVITY ON THE GO
DINOSAURS
Tyrannosaur, pterosaur, pliosaur, ROAR!
Nothing's more awesome than a dinosaur.
There are SMALL ONES and BIG ONES and FIERCE ONES and more!
In this book you'll find stickers and stencils and doodles galore!
The biggest dinosaur fan ever is:
(write your name here)

# WHAT'S INSIDE THIS BOOK?

## COLOUR AND CREATE

Think, create, draw, imagine! There are oodles of doodles and colouring activities.

## STICKERS

There are dinosaur stickers at the back of the book. Use them for the sticker activities, to create cool scenes, or just stick them everywhere!

## STENCILS

There's a sheet of stencils at the back of the book that you can take out and use.

## PUZZLES AND QUIZZES

Spot the difference, join the dots, navigate the mazes plus much more. Then try the ultimate dinosaur quiz at the end.

## THINGS TO MAKE AND DO

Keep busy for hours by building a Giganotosaurus, making a mobile and creating a flipbook. Get creative with some scaly art paper, too.

CARLTON KIDS

This is a Carlton book.
Text, design and illustration
© Carlton Books 2015

Published in 2016 by
Carlton Books Limited,
an imprint of the Carlton Publishing Group,
20 Mortimer Street, London, W1T 3JW.

ISBN: 978-1-78312-184-7
Printed and bound in China

AUTHOR: Penny Worms
ILLUSTRATIONS: Liza Lewis and Anna Stiles
DESIGNER: Ceri Hurst
DESIGN MANAGER: Emily Clarke
EXECUTIVE EDITOR: Anna Brett
PRODUCTION: Marion Storz

PICTURE CREDITS
All background textures and patterns supplied by Thinkstock.com

# THE TIME MACHINE

We are going back in time to around
165 million years ago – well before humans lived on the planet.
We are heading to a land where dinosaurs ruled, huge flying reptiles
soared overhead and gigantic sea creatures terrorized the seas.

ARE YOU READY? HERE WE GO...

Draw yourself
inside this
time machine.

Anyone you
want to take
with you?

# DINOSAUR HALL OF FAME

Here are portraits of some famous dinosaurs.
Complete the pictures and colour them in.

- TITANIC -
THE BIGGEST T. REX

Titanic is the largest of all
the T. rexes. And his teeth
are the biggest too!

- MINI -
THE SMALLEST
MICRORAPTOR

Mini is so tiny, she lives
in fear of being trampled on by
any passing dinosaur. She's only
40cm long – that's not much
longer than a ruler!

- EINSTEIN -
THE CLEVEREST STEGOSAURUS

Stegosauruses are not known for
their brains. Einstein is different.
He can outwit any dinosaur.

- ALVERA -
THE KINDEST ALLOSAURUS

Alvera is laughed at by her Allosaurus
friends because she's friendly not fierce. She
likes being kind to dinosaurs in need.

## - SUNNY -
### THE HAPPIEST TRICERATOPS

Most Triceratops males are grumpy all the time. Sunny was born happy and he's stayed like that. No one ever picks a fight with him.

## - VELOCITY -
### THE FASTEST VELOCIRAPTOR

Velocity can outrun any Velociraptor and any predators. She is the Jurassic world champion sprinter!

## - DUSTBIN -
### THE HUNGRIEST DIPLODOCUS

There isn't a tree, shrub or fern that Dustbin won't eat. He even eats stones to help him digest all that veggie food. TIP: Never stand downwind. Stinky!!

## - GRANDDAD -
### THE OLDEST IGUANODON

No one knows of a dinosaur older than Granddad. He's seen it all – volcanic eruptions, meteor strikes, extinctions, but he's still going strong.

# WHERE'S MY ARMOUR?

Terrifying Rex is on the prowl!
Quick, draw these smaller dinosaurs
something to protect themselves from him.

WHAT'S FOR DINNER?
This dinosaur has an empty plate.
Draw him a delicious dinner.
Meat-eater or plant-eater?
Ketchup or mayo?
Fruit juice or pond water?
Napkin or… don't be daft, dinosaurs don't use napkins!

# SPOT THE DIFFERENCE

Can you spot the ten differences between these two dinosaur pictures?

 Answers are at the back of the book. 

# WELCOME TO DINOSAUR ISLAND

Find the dinosaur stickers that match
the shapes to see who lives where.
Use the clues to help you.

## TALLTREE FOREST
A dinosaur with plates
on its back lives here
and eats the juicy ferns.

## THE RANGE
A huge dinosaur
with a long neck and
tail lives here.

## THE RUSHING RIVER
A fish-eating
dinosaur lives
here.

## THE ROCKFACE
A flying reptile has
its nest here.

## THE TRIASSIC TRENCH
A scary sea monster
lives here.

Answers are at the back of the book.

# FABULOUS FOSSIL FIND

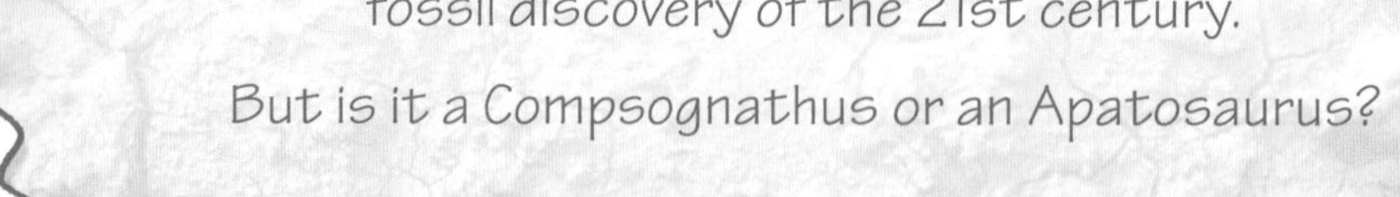

Eureka! You have found the most fascinating
fossil discovery of the 21st century.

But is it a Compsognathus or an Apatosaurus?

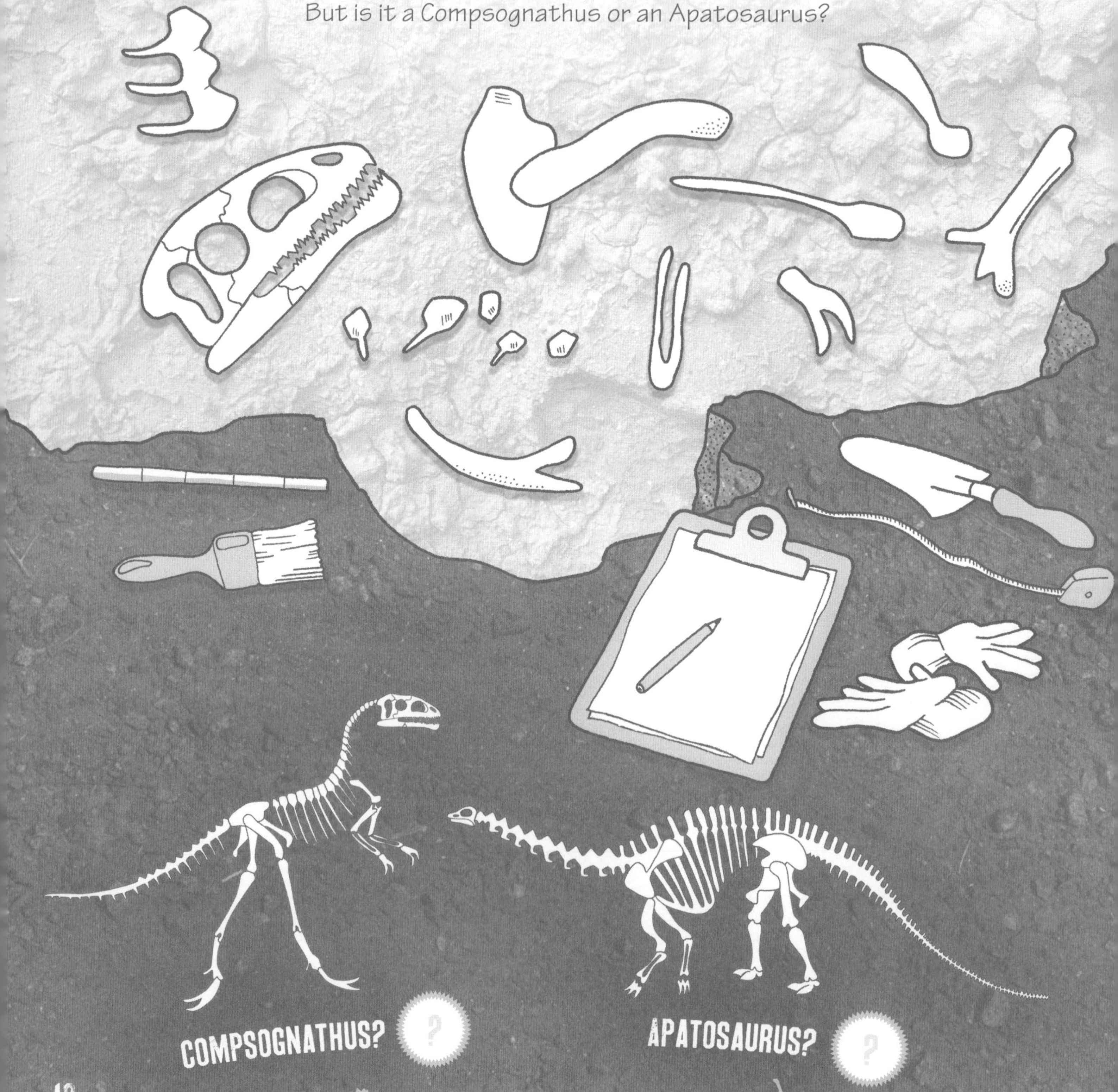

COMPSOGNATHUS? ?

APATOSAURUS? ?



Answer is at the back of the book.

# NAME THAT DINOSAUR

Imagine getting to name your
very own dinosaur.

You could name him after yourself
(Ollyraptor?)

You could name him after where you live
(Manchestersaurus?)

You could name him after his extraordinary
dinosaur features (Duospikotops?)

Or you could just come up with the silliest,
scariest name imaginable!

# THE GREAT COLOUR CONTEST

What colours dinosaurs were is still a big mystery to humans.
Colour in these Oviraptors however you like –
blue, green or fluorescent pink!

Dinosaur crests were probably as bright as
birds' crests, so go colour crazy!

# BUILD A GIGANOTOSAURUS

Giganotosaurus was a REALLY BIG
meat-eating dinosaur – just what you
need in your bedroom!

TURN OVER TO SEE
HOW TO MAKE IT.

# 1

Ask an adult to help you cut out the four pieces below.

# 2

Glue them onto a piece of cardboard.

# 3

Ask your adult to cut around the pieces again, and snip along the four dotted lines.

# 4

Colour the blank side in however you want. You could stick on some art paper (see pages 40 or 72).

# 5

Slot the legs onto the body and the feet into the legs... ROAR! There you have your dinosaur!

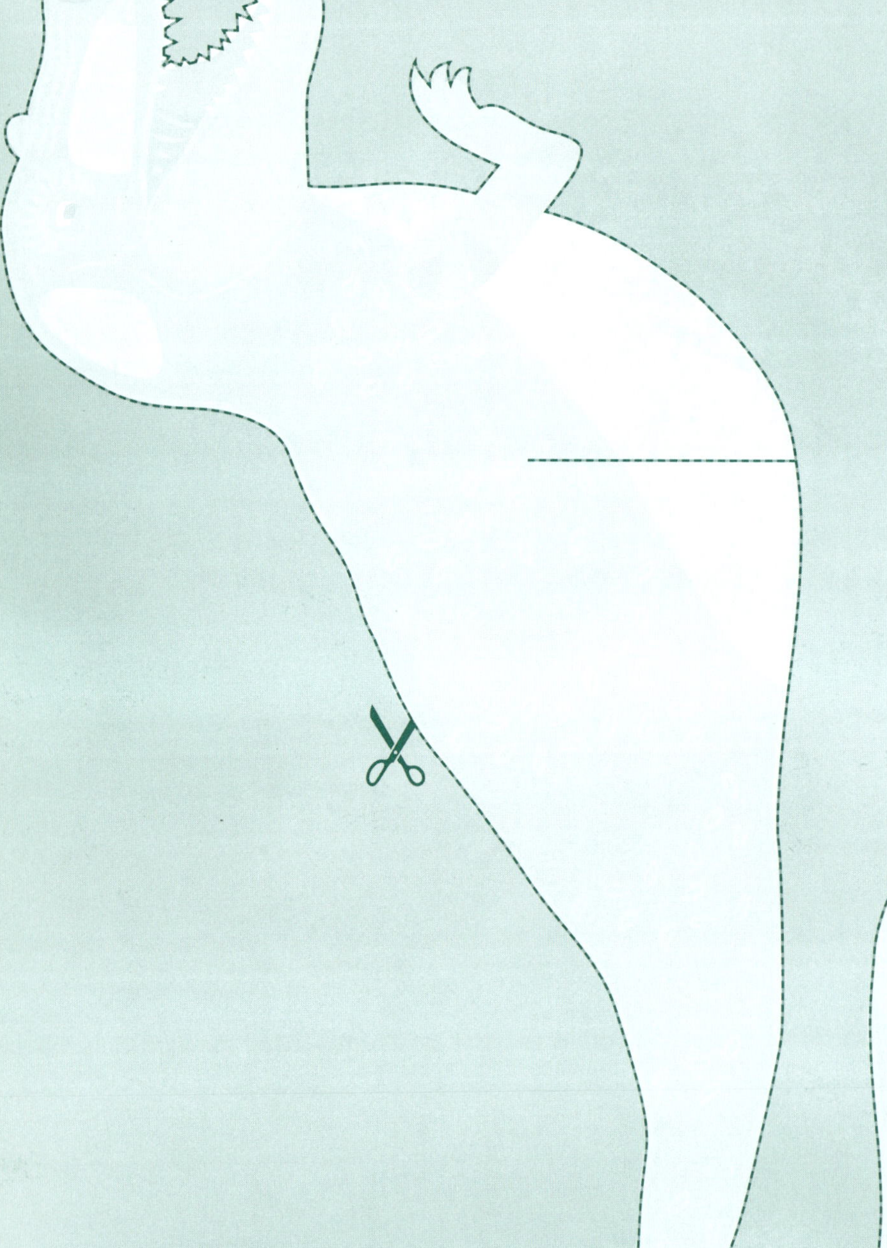

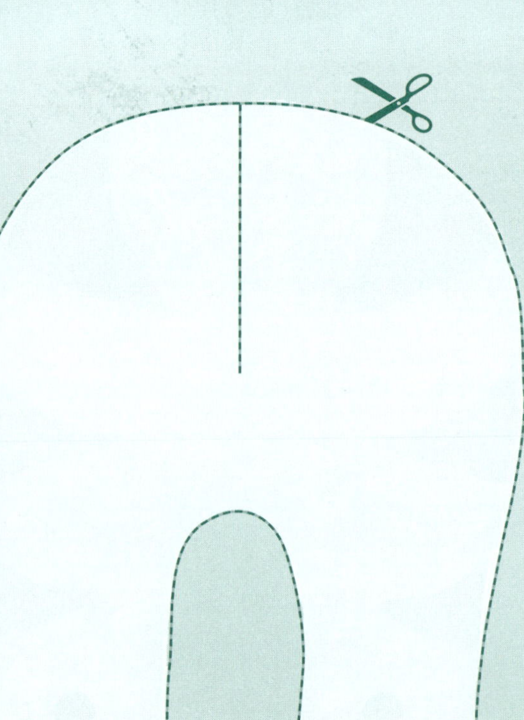

# DOT-TO-DOT DINOSAUR

Connect the dots to reveal a
dangerous dinosaur – if you dare!

Answer is at the back of the book.

# MATCH UP

Match the dinosaur
to its description.

BARYONYX
I have a mouth like a
crocodile and big curved
claws on my little hands.

ARCHAEOPTERYX
I'm proof that birds
probably did descend
from dinosaurs.

DICERATOPS
I'm the cousin of
Triceratops.

SAUROPELTA
I'm like an armadillo
with extra spiky
neck armour.

Answers are at the back of the book.

# DINO SCRAMBLE

The names of five dinosaurs have got mixed up below. Can you unscramble the letters and draw a line to the correct dinosaur image on the right?

RTXE

ASLRUUSOLOA

TGSESOARUSU

PICVETLRROAO

RTCAPSEORIT

# HOW TO **DRAW A TYRANNOSAUR**

Copy each of the drawing steps into the box below.

**1** Start with a shape like a baked bean. See how the bottom end is wider than the top end.

**2** Now add the two legs. You'll need to rub out the bottom of your original shape. This dinosaur has three toes on each foot.

**3** Next you're adding the two arms. They are a lot smaller than the legs and have three fingers.

**4** Concentrate when adding the head. It's easiest to start with an oval shape and then draw in the open mouth.

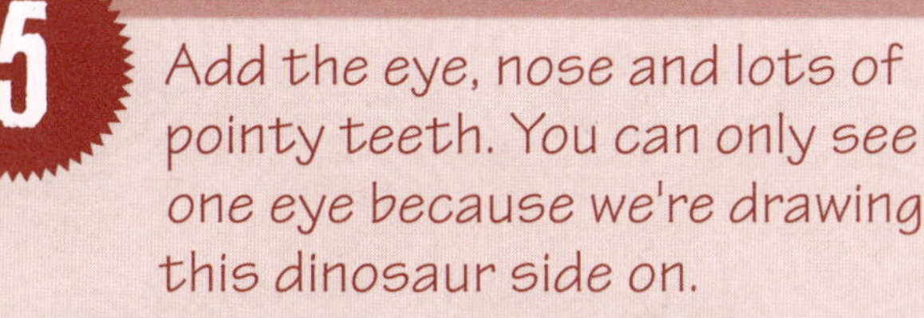

**5** Add the eye, nose and lots of pointy teeth. You can only see one eye because we're drawing this dinosaur side on.

**6** Finally, add the large tail and draw a line to show where his tummy is. Colour him in and think of a name!

## DRAW YOUR TYRANNOSAUR HERE

# SHIPWRECK!

Circle the pictures and fill in the gaps to make up your own prehistoric adventure story.

I had been travelling on a ship called the ..................................

We were having a yummy dinner, when suddenly we were hit by a ..................................

The next thing I knew, I was washed up on a strange island called ..................................

The first creature I saw was a ..................................

I ran as fast as I could ..................................

But ..................................

..................................

..................................

(Finish the story yourself!)

# DOOR HANGER

Turn over to find out what to do next.

# HOW TO MAKE YOUR DOOR HANGER

**1**

Ask an adult to help you cut out these two hanger shapes.

**2**

Stick the two backs together to make one hanger.

**3**

Hang it on your door. Turn it round to tell visitors if they are allowed to come in or not!

# BE A FOSSIL HUNTER

Fossils are fascinating and very hard to find.
Are you a budding fossil hunter?
Answer these questions to find out.

**1** FOSSILS ARE USUALLY FOUND IN:
- **A** soft, sedimentary rocks
- **B** shiny, hard rocks

**2** THE BEST PLACE TO LOOK FOR THEM IS:
- **A** on the beach
- **B** in the fridge

**3** IN LITTLE ROCKS, YOU MIGHT FIND:
- **A** an ammonite
- **B** an allosaurus

**4** IN BIG FLAT ROCKS, YOU MIGHT FIND:
- **A** a dinosaur footprint
- **B** a living dinosaur

**5** FOSSILS ARE FORMED WHEN:
- **A** a creature dies and gets covered up by mud, sand or rock
- **B** a creature gets stuck up a tree

A is the correct answer to all the questions.

If you answered mostly As, you were born to be a fossil hunter!

If you answered mostly Bs, you need to get studying!

23

# DINOSAUR EGGS

Shhhhh! You've found a nest of dinosaur eggs.

# HIDE-AND-SEEK

These five dinosaur friends are playing hide-and-seek.
Can you find them? Circle them when you spot them.

Add stickers of other friends who want to play.



Answers are at the back of the book.

# STICKER SNAP

Find the stickers that match these dinosaur shapes.

Answers are at the back of the book.

# DINO-DOODLE-OO

Here are some terrible teeth, eerie eyes,
scary spikes and huge claws.
Draw who they belong to!

# PTEROSAURS GALORE

Here are some huge flying reptiles called pterosaurs.
How many can you count?
Draw one more or add a sticker.

Answer is at the back of the book.

# MAKE A MASK

Turn over to find out what to do next...

# HOW TO MAKE YOUR DINOSAUR MASK

**1** Ask an adult to help you cut out the mask.

**2** Cut out the eye holes and the little holes on the side.

**3** Put the mask against your face and measure a length of string or elastic to fit around your head.

**4** Tie the elastic or string through the little holes.

**5** Put your mask on and start stomping around the room like a dinosaur!

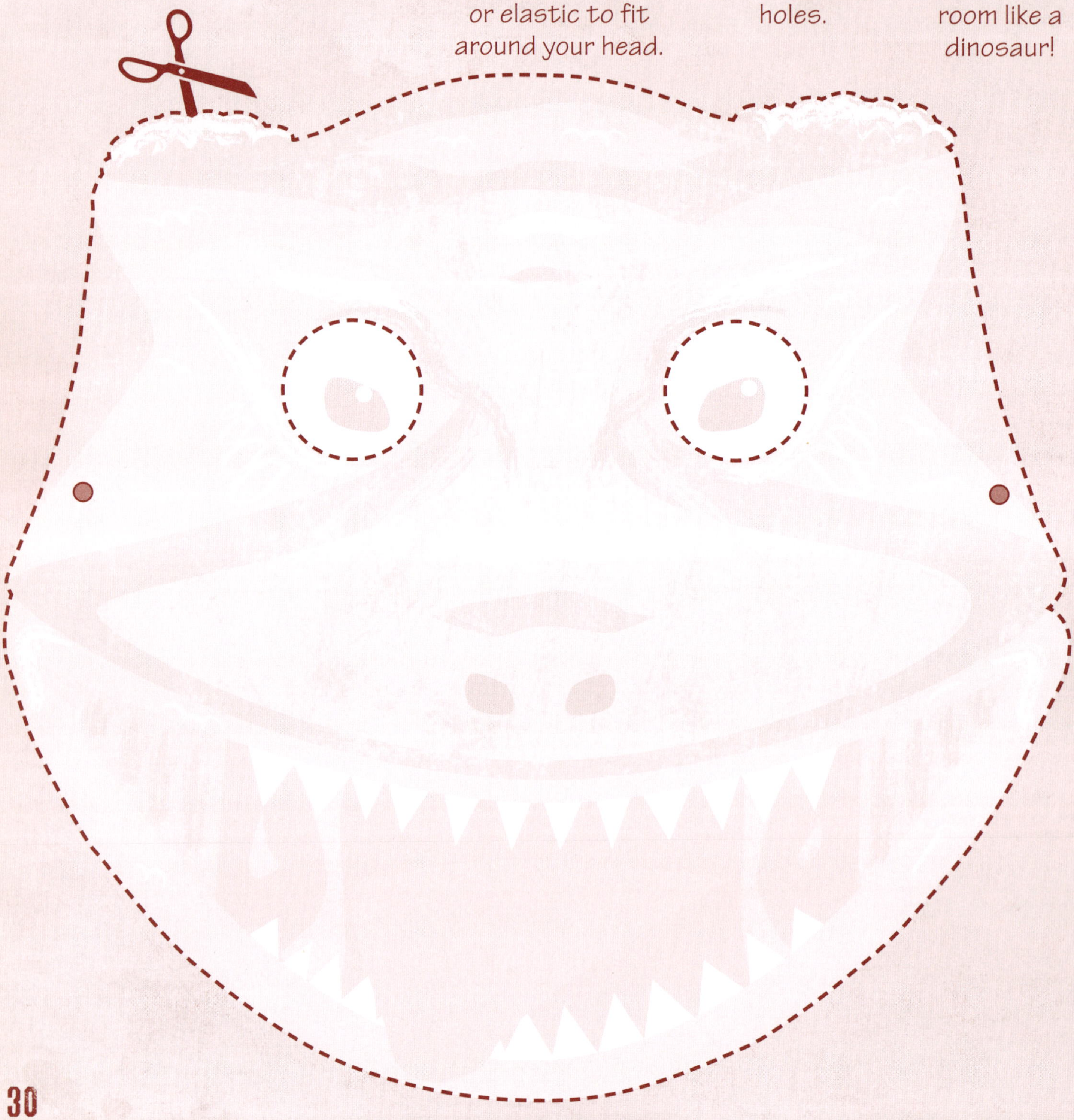

QUICK, RUN!
Help this little dinosaur escape the angry Allosaurus by choosing the right path to his burrow.
C
A
B
SAFE
31
Answer is at the back of the book.

# CRETACEOUS CREEK

Use your stencils, stickers, pens and pencils to create a busy scene.

Who's flying in the sky?
Who's swimming in the creek?

# IT'S A MIXED-UP LIFE

From egg to grown-up dinosaur,
put these pictures in order.

**A**

**B**

**C**

**D**

Answer is at the back of the book.

# ERUPTION!

This volcano is about to erupt. 3, 2, 1, Go! Make it blow!

What's this dinosaur saying?

Draw a cave to protect the nest.

# COPY TO COMPLETE

Using the right-side of the picture as a guide,
complete then colour the picture.

# HADROSAUR-WHO?

Find the stickers that match these strange-headed dinosaurs.

Answers are at the back of the book.

# SKIN, SCALES AND BEAUTIFUL TAILS

On the next few pages, you'll find patterned paper to add some colour details to your dinosaurs. Here's what to do with it...

**1**

Cut out the paper and use it to add colour to your dinosaurs on pages 14, 35, 36 and 43.

**2**

Use your stencils to draw dino shapes on your art paper, then cut them out to create a dramatic dinosaur scene.

**3**

Use the paper for anything you like! Customize a notebook, do dinosaur origami, or make a dinosaur mobile for your room (see page 70).

# PARASAUROLOPHUS PARADE

What did they look like?
Nobody knows!
So create your own with
whatever patterns and
colours you like.

# TERRIBLE TWINS

## IVAN THE INCREDIBLE

There are **12 DIFFERENCES** between these two T. rex twins.
Can you find them?

# TERENCE THE TERRIBLE

Answers are at the back of the book.

# HOW TO **DRAW A PTEROSAUR**

Copy each of the drawing steps into the box below.

**1** Begin with two lines for the wings. Notice that they are not straight lines, they have a kink in the middle.

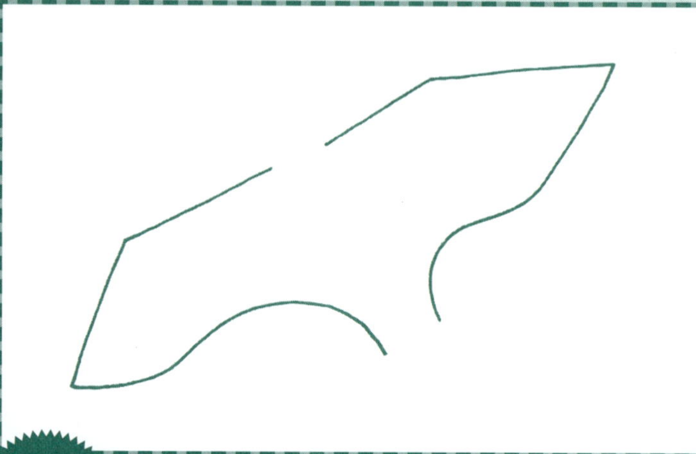

**2** Next you need to draw two curvy lines to make the wing shapes. Use a pencil in case you make a mistake and need to rub it out.

**3** Copy these lines to draw the neck, body and a thin pointy tail.

**4** Now add the arms and legs. The arms are long and thin and have three fingers. The legs are shorter with two toes.

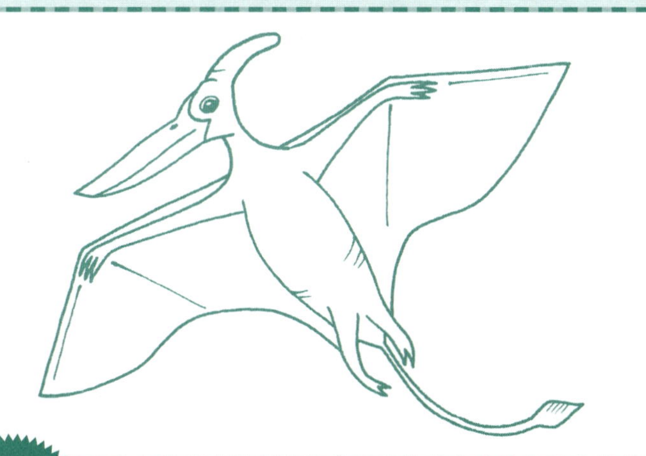

**5** Time to give your pterosaur a head. He's got a long beak, a pointed head crest and a large eye.

**6** Finishing touches include detail on the wings, body and tip of the tail. Then add colour!

## DRAW YOUR PTEROSAUR HERE

# IF DINOSAURS WERE ALIVE TODAY

Here is a city scene. Add in some dinosaurs...
then some people... and then lots of panic!

FIND THE FOSSILS
How many ammonites can you count in this picture?
WRITE YOUR ANSWER HERE.
?
Answer is at the back of the book.
49

**1**

Carefully cut out the pages of your flipbook along the dotted lines.

**2**

Stack them together, making sure the numbers are in the top left corner with 1 at the top to 18 at the bottom.

**3**

Pick up the stack and tap it on a hard surface on the right edge – this is where you flip the pages, so they need to be aligned perfectly.

**4**

Holding the stack firmly together, secure it on the left edge with a bulldog clip.

**5**

Now hold the bulldog clip with your left hand, and flip the pages with your right hand for some funny dinosaur action.

**6**

You can draw and make your own flipbook on the reverse of the pages.

DINOSAUR ROAR!
ROAR, squawk, GROWL or grumble.
What noises are these dinosaurs making?
Use fun lettering to write it in the speech bubbles.
53

# FRIENDLY OR FRIGHTENING?

Finish drawing these dinosaurs' faces – add eyes, eyebrows and mouths. Give them expressions to show whether they are smiley or scary!

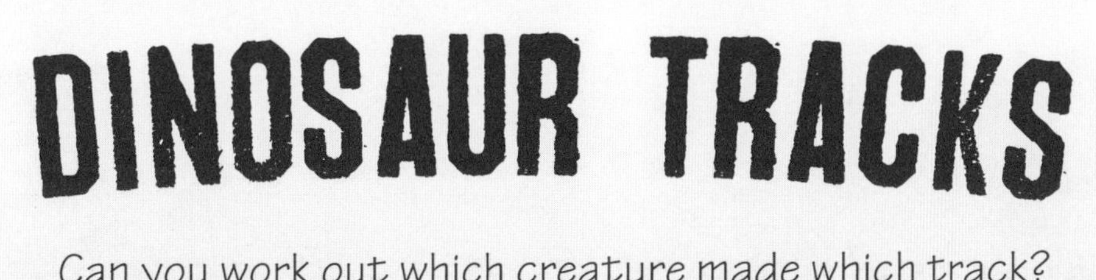

# DINOSAUR TRACKS

Can you work out which creature made which track?
Write the correct letter next to each dinosaur.

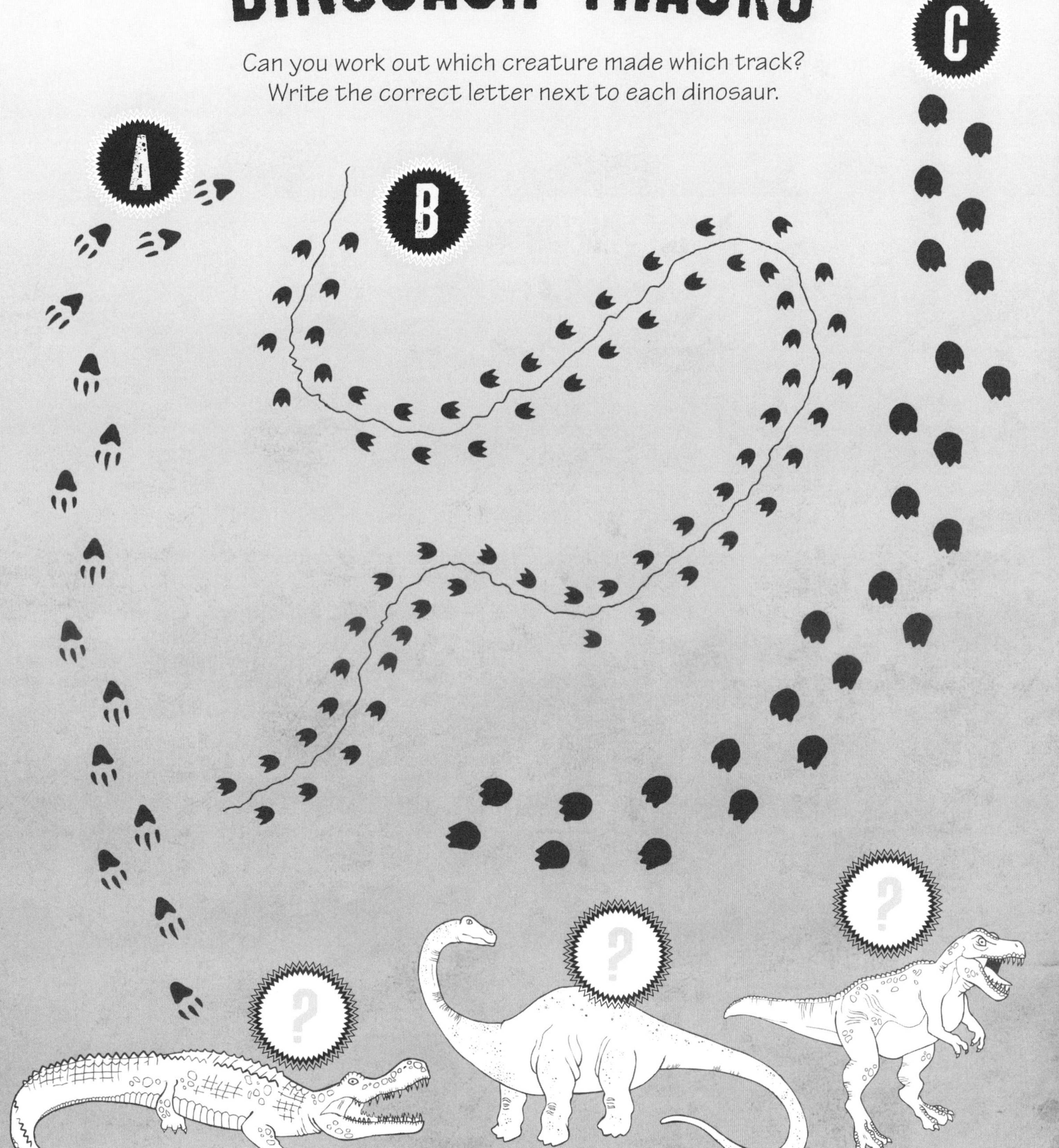

A

B

C

?

?

?

# CONTINENTS DIVIDE

When dinosaurs ruled the world, it was very different. There were no continents, such as Africa or America. All the land was joined together. When it started to break up, it looked like this...

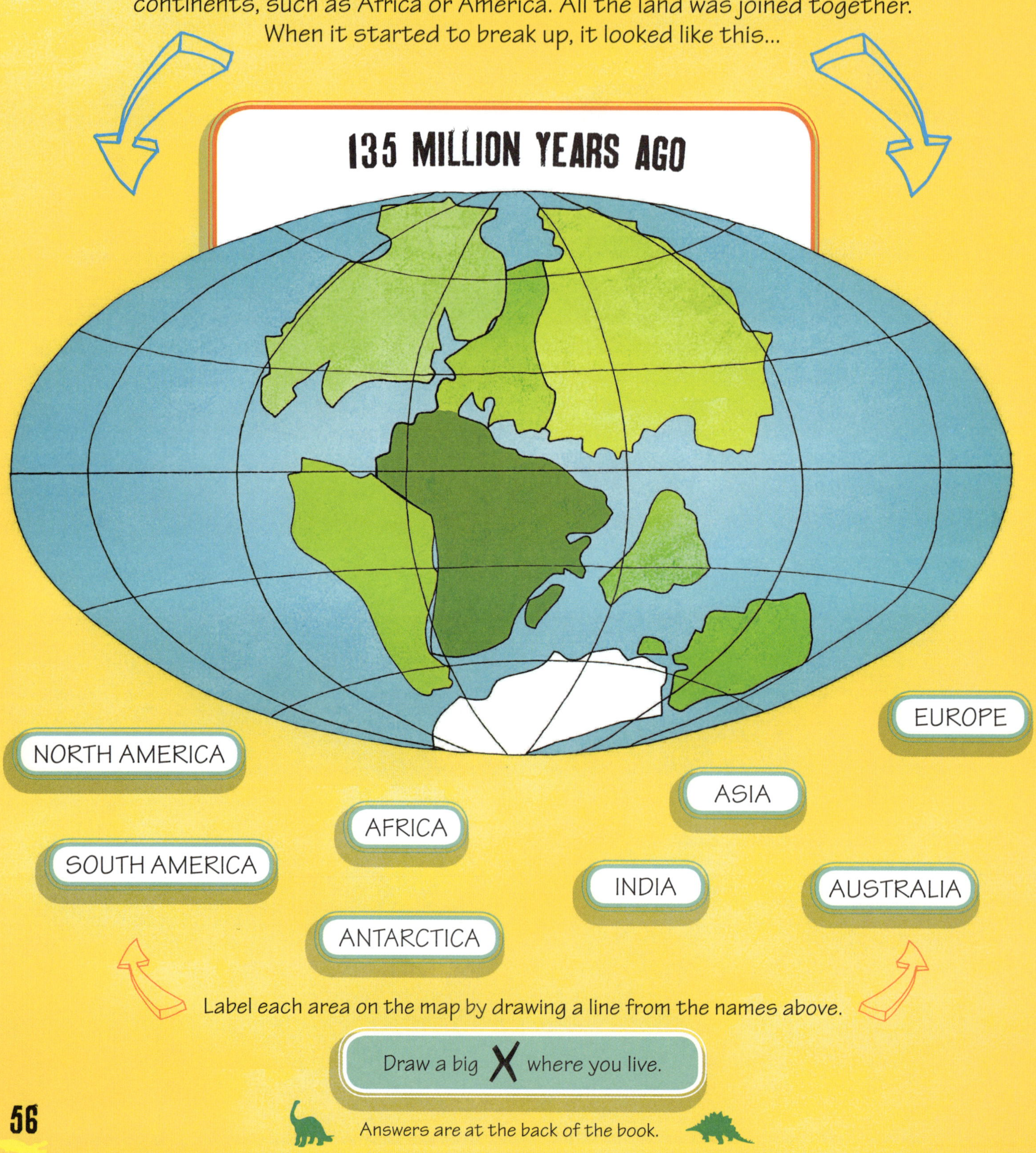


Label each area on the map by drawing a line from the names above.

Draw a big X where you live.



Answers are at the back of the book.

# MATCH UP

Can you match the dinosaur with its description?

**1**

**2**

**3**

**4**

## B
### ARGENTINOSAURUS
Dinosaurs don't get much
bigger than me!
I am a huge plant-eater
with a long neck and tail.

?

## D
### STRUTHIOMIMUS
I look like an ostrich,
with long legs. I can run
faster than
a racehorse.

?

## A
### COMPSOGNATHUS
I'm a very small dinosaur
with a long snout. I love
hunting for lizards to eat.

?

## C
### STEGOCERAS
I use my strong skull as
a battering ram against
rival stegocerases.

?

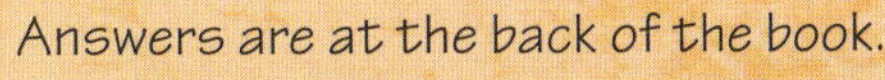

Answers are at the back of the book.

# IN THE RING

Angry Al the Allosaurus is a champion fighter. Here are three possible opponents.
Draw one of them in the boxing ring, then fill in the score card.
Tick who wins each round. Then write in who gets the knockout!

# WHAT'S IN A NAME?

All dinosaur names have a meaning. How many do you know?
See if you can match these names with their meaning.
Look at the shape of the dinosaurs for clues.

SPINOSAURUS

TYRANNOSAURUS REX

ANKLYOSAURUS

OVIRAPTOR

TRICERATOPS

TROODON

## MEANINGS

| | | |
|---|---|---|
| Spine lizard | Wounding tooth | King of the tyrant reptiles |
| Egg thief | Three-horned face | Fused lizard |

 Answers are at the back of the book. 

# DINO SPOTTING

Add some more dinosaurs into this Jurassic forest.
Draw them in using your stencils, or add stickers.

# DINOSAUR DREAMS

Suchomimus is having a snooze. Is he dreaming of a feast of his favourite fish? A beautiful Suchomimus lady? You decide and draw it in!

# STICKER SNAP

Find the stickers that match these dinosaur shadows.

Answers are at the back of the book.

# DEINOSUCHUS DOT-TO-DOT

Join the dots to see the beast
attacking this dinosaur!



Answer is at the back of the book.

# WATER BABIES

These baby ichthyosaurs have just been born.
They need to get to the surface to breathe.
Can you find a path for them through the kelp forest?

Answer is at the back of the book.

# PLESIOSAURUS PARADISE

Look at this group of plesiosaurs.
How many can you count?

Answer is at the back of the book.

# HOW TO **DRAW A MOSASAURUS**

Copy each of the drawing steps into the box below.

**1** To start your Mosasaurus you need to draw an S shape with a long curve at the top looping all the way round to the bottom. Then rub out the lines where shown in the image above.

**2** Next you need to draw in two flippers. Notice how one is bigger than the other.

**3** Add the head by drawing two triangle shapes and then adding lines to create the open mouth.

**4** Now for some fun! Add lots of sharp teeth and pointy spikes.

**5** Give your Mosasaurus an eye with some lines around it to make him look fierce. Add some spots on the flippers.

**6** Finish by adding lines on the body to show his skin then decide what colour you're going to make it.

## DRAW YOUR MOSASAURUS HERE

# AN UNDERWATER WORLD

While dinosaurs were roaming the land, many huge swimming reptiles were ruling the seas. Add more to this scene using stickers and stencils, or draw your own.

Are there any fish for them to eat?
Jellyfish or squid?

# MAKE A MOBILE

The next pages contain more patterned paper – so get creative! If you want to make a dinosaur mobile for your room, here's what to do.

**1.** Cut out the dinosaur templates on the opposite page, or ask an adult to help you.

**2.** Draw around these shapes to make more dinosaurs on any leftover paper.

**3.** Cut them out. The more the better as you can make multiple mobiles!

**4.** Ask an adult to make little holes at the top of each dinosaur shape.

**5.** Thread some cotton through these holes, securing it with tape.

**6.** Tie your dinosaurs to a coat hanger, and hang it somewhere in your room.

# WHAT'S IN A WORD?

Look at the word

## palaeontologist

How many words can you make from the letters in it?

Words must be three letters or more.
If you find more than 12, go to the top of the class.

HERE ARE A COUPLE OF EXAMPLES...
plant   lion   ant

*Pssst... Palaeontologist means someone who studies fossils.*

Colour this star gold
if you find any to do
with dinosaurs
(think body parts!).

# THE BIG DINOSAUR QUIZ

How much do you know about dinosaurs?
Let's find out.

**1 WHAT IS A SAUROPOD?**
A) A place where dinosaurs used to sleep
B) A large plant-eater with a long neck
C) A plant that dinosaurs used to eat

**2 SPINOSAURUS WAS**
A) Big
B) Small
C) Able to fly

**3** Tyrannosaurus and Spinosaurus used to fight all the time. True or False?

**4 WHAT IS A COPROLITE?**
A) Fossilized dinosaur poo
B) A person who owns a dinosaur skeleton
C) A baby dinosaur

**5 WHAT CREATURES ARE DESCENDED FROM DINOSAURS?**
A) Snakes
B) Monkeys
C) Birds

76

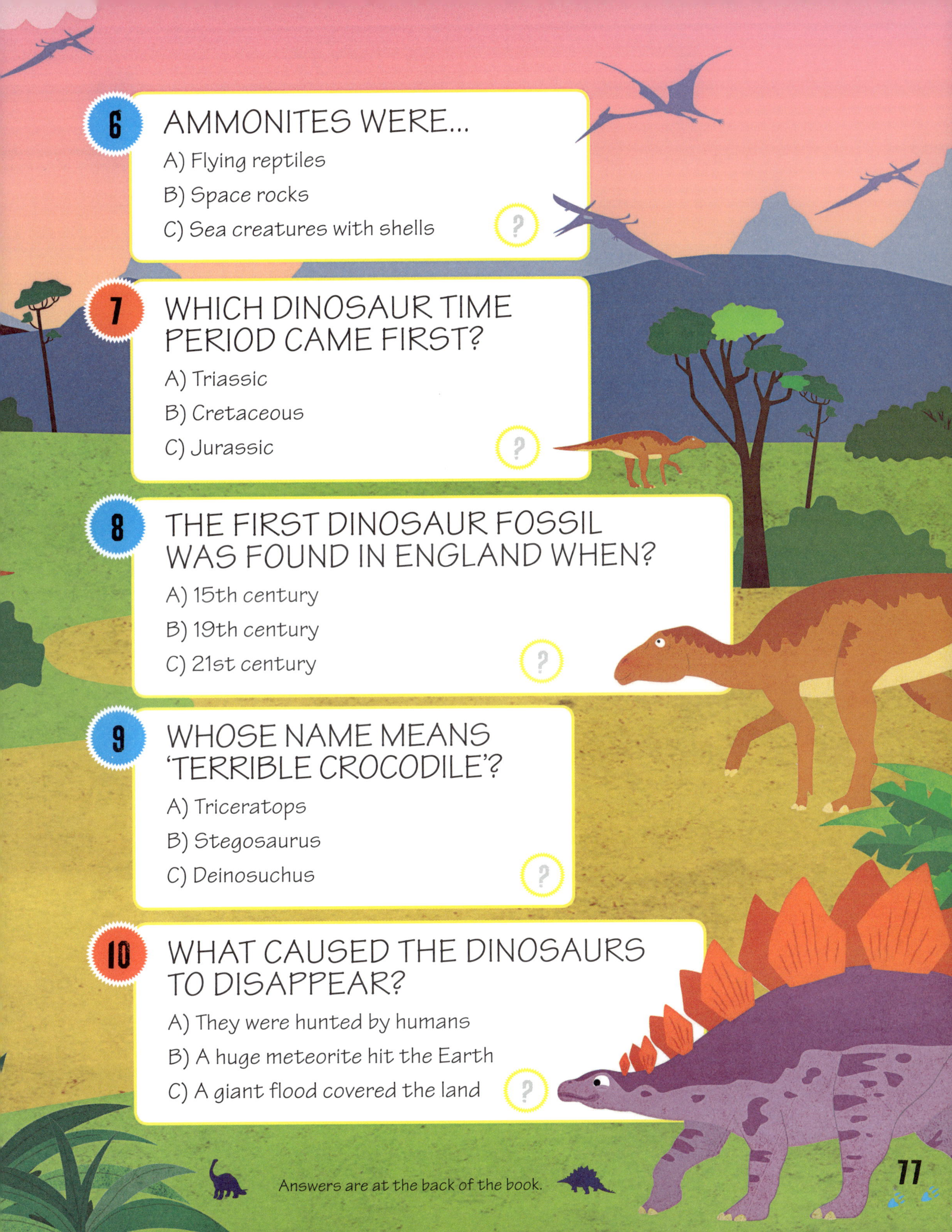

**6** AMMONITES WERE...

A) Flying reptiles

B) Space rocks

C) Sea creatures with shells

**7** WHICH DINOSAUR TIME PERIOD CAME FIRST?

A) Triassic

B) Cretaceous

C) Jurassic

**8** THE FIRST DINOSAUR FOSSIL WAS FOUND IN ENGLAND WHEN?

A) 15th century

B) 19th century

C) 21st century

**9** WHOSE NAME MEANS 'TERRIBLE CROCODILE'?

A) Triceratops

B) Stegosaurus

C) Deinosuchus

**10** WHAT CAUSED THE DINOSAURS TO DISAPPEAR?

A) They were hunted by humans

B) A huge meteorite hit the Earth

C) A giant flood covered the land

Answers are at the back of the book.

# DINOSAUR DECLARATION

My favourite dinosaur is:

........................................................

Its name means:

........................................................

Carnivore (meat-eater)
or herbivore (plant-eater)?

........................................................

The colour I think it was is:

........................................................

The best thing about it is:

........................................................

# Certificate of membership

This certifies that

........................................................................

is a totally brilliant fossil hunter
and dinosaur expert.

Signed by

*Dr. Phineas Buckland*

DR. PHINEAS BUCKLAND

(descendant of the first-ever dinosaur hunter)

THE ANSWERS!

8
9
10
COMPSOGNATHUS
15

16
SAUROPELTA
BARYONYX
DICERATOPS
ARCHAEOPTERYX

17
T. REX
ALLOSAURUS
STEGOSAURUS
VELOCIRAPTOR
TRICERATOPS

25
26
Where did they go?
I think they went this way.
What's that noise?
Quick! Hide!

28
THERE ARE
11

31
A
B
C
SAFE

34
B
C
D
A
B  C  D  A

37
45

49
THERE ARE
19

55
B
C
A

56
135 MILLION YEARS AGO
NORTH AMERICA
AFRICA
SOUTH AMERICA
ANTARCTICA
EUROPE
ASIA
INDIA
AUSTRALIA

57
B  ARGENTINOSAURUS
C  STEGOCERAS
D  STRUTHIOMIMUS
A  COMPSOGNATHUS

59
Spinosaurus  Spine lizard
Tyrannosaurus rex  King of the tyrant reptiles
Anklyosaurus  Fused lizard
Troodon  Wounding tooth
Oviraptor  Egg thief
Triceratops  Three-horned face

62

63
64
FINISH
START

65
THERE ARE
18

76-77
1  B      2  A
3  True   4  A    5  C
6  C      7  A    8  B
9  C      10  B